CW01475582

BUSINESS RELATIONSHIPS:
KEY TO YOUR SUCCESS

THOMAS S. ENRIGHT

i

Produced by:

FriesenPress
Suite 300 – 852 Fort Street
Victoria, BC, Canada V8W 1H8

www.friesenpress.com

Distributed to the trade by The Ingram Book Company

BABE / ALEX
All the Best
Enjoy Tam

Table of Contents

We all have a number of business relationships. But, have we ever stopped and asked ourselves *Why do we have the relationships we do?* Have these relationships progressed to the appropriate or needed level? And, are there other relationships we should have?

Typically our relationships have happened almost by accident, and are usually with business colleagues we like—or, at the very least, those that are like-minded to us.

In *Business Relationships: Key to Your Success,* we examine the power of having the *right* level of relationships, at the *right* time, with the *right* people, from all our company's stakeholder groups. This is called the "Three Right Rule."

Imagine the impact of the Three Right Rule on our corporate branding, reputation management, crisis preparedness, strategic and annual business planning, new product development, research, risk management and, of course, decision-making.

Think of the effect this would have on our own career.

The good news is, unlike many other self-help, self-improvement processes that require a significant amount of time, effort and money to implement, *Business Relationships: Key to Your Success* can be quickly, easily and inexpensively put into action. That's right, the amount of change and cost required to achieve all of these benefits is not significant. It simply requires a modification from our current approach to relationships to a more pro-active, strategic approach.

Unfortunately, the closest many of us ever come to realizing the power of strategic relationship management occurs when we face a crisis or major issue/event.

It is at that moment when we realize we do not have the relationships we need in place with the right stakeholder/s in order to deal as effectively as possible with the crisis or major issue. Or, we learn the relationship/s we have in place are not with the right people or at the right level.

In typical fashion, we swear never to let this happen again with this particular stakeholder—but very rarely do we stop and consider the weakness in our overall approach to strategic relationship management across ALL stakeholder groups.

In effect, we are setting ourselves up to repeat our unpleasant experience again in the future with another stakeholder.

Many times, we believe we have much stronger relationships than we actually do, and when it comes to relationships it's the case of One Size Fits All.

In *Business Relationships: Key to Your Success,* we explore the various levels of relationships and what differentiates one level from the next. Understanding the correct level of relationship we have with our various stakeholders and how to progress these relationships to the right level is key to your success.

The question is, if you are not pro-active and strategic about your relationships, is someone else? It's reasonable to consider how a competitor could use strategic relationship management as a secret weapon against your company.

The good news is that it is never too late to improve your game when it comes to strategic relationship management. All it takes is for one person to experience the power and benefits of strategic relationship management to begin to make a difference.

And, while it is not necessary for strategic relationship management to be a corporate-wide objective, the more people engaged in the program, the greater the benefit to your company.

Business Relationships: Key to Your Success outlines a significant competitive advantage that is easily within your grasp—and requires little change or cost to produce significant results.

To Linda, Matthew (and Lauren), Courtney (and Noah) and Piper,
my most important relationships

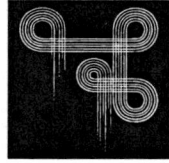

Preface

One of the things I have always found challenging about so called "self help" books is that the magnitude of the change is often too great to be able to make it a sustainable long-term behaviour.

Rarely have I been able to make the required change and, therefore, could not realize the potential gain.

Sometimes, the required change involved a complete organizational change that would take significant time, cost and effort to enact. Again, the opportunity would be lost.

The good news about this book is that, while the size of change is not overwhelming, the impact is significant. It is based on the fact that we already have a number of business relationships and, therefore, bring an existing level of expertise to the table. In this book we will expand on this existing expertise and formalize the process of determining with whom to build relationships, and what type of relationship to build in order to achieve success. Many of today's business management courses and books tell us, as managers, to control the things we can control and not to dwell on the things that are out of our control. *Business Relationships: Key to Your Success* shows you how to take strategic control of your relationships for maximum benefit.

The second piece of good news is that the ideas in this book can be applied individually, within a group, or across an entire company.

In the case of my own personal journey, strategic relationship management has played an extremely important role in my success. I have worked for four different organizations so far in my career with the last two jobs at the President and CEO level. I realized while writing this book that I never applied for any of these jobs.

My first and fourth jobs came as a direct result of my senior relationship network. I was headhunted for my second and third jobs and learned after the fact that my name had been put forward to the head hunters by someone from my relationship network.

I should also state that I have never created a relationship with the sole intent of getting a job. My career has happened, to a large part, because of my approach to relationship management.

At the very least, if this book causes you to build at least one new relationship or rethink an existing relationship because of its potential strategic value, then I would deem that a success. If you take it beyond that basic level, then I will be delighted.

Enjoy!

Acknowledgements

I have been blessed throughout my career to work with many amazing people who directly or indirectly have taught me many things.

Someone once said "you can always use a good editor". David Milliken was not only a good editor for *Business Relationships: Key to Your Success*, he also strongly believes in the power of relationships.

Early in my career I was fortunate enough to have two mentors: Dorothy Hardman and John Thornton, both of whom played critical roles in shaping my approach to business.

My late father-in-law, Len Rasberry, showed me, before I started my business career, what integrity and respect meant in business.

Through his ongoing encouragement, Paul Potts (President and CEO of the Press Association of the UK – retired) taught me how to deal with challenging issues in a supportive way. Paul also demonstrated to me the art of determining when relationships were needed and what was involved in creating high-level relationships with senior executives.

The numerous illustrations in this book help communicate the various messages. I extend a special thank you to Noah Conti for his creativity and expertise in bringing these images to life. For more information about Noah's work, please visit his website at pixelepic.com.

"It's All About Relationships" – Who Knew?

As I was being introduced at the beginning of a workshop I was conducting for a healthcare company, one of the company co-founder's stated that, in her opinion, success in their business was "all about relationships".

It was a powerful way to begin the workshop and certainly got the participant's attention. But it was not the first time I had heard such a phrase from business colleagues and acquaintances.

Even with the company co-founder's strong statement regarding the importance of relationships, once we had completed the workshop and brought even more analysis, thought and focus onto the level of their relationships, the need to increase their pro-active, strategic relationship management became clearer and more critical to their success.

As this healthcare company was B2B (business-to-business) one may think the "all about relationships" statement was perfectly justified. However, since a well-executed strategic relationship management program extends far beyond a company's client base to include all key stakeholder groups, *all* types of business benefit. Regardless of whether your company is B2B or B2C (business-to-consumer), strategic relationship management will have a direct, positive effect on your success.

The world of relationships has three dimensions: One is the *social dimension* which would include our relationships with friends, neighbours, church congregations, sport team mates, etc. There is also a *family-based* dimension to relationships which would include

1

immediate and extended family members. The third dimension is based on *business relationships*. While it is business relationships this body of work is based upon, the impact that *all* of our relationships have on our lives deserves recognition. A social worker who was a guest speaker at an event I once attended summed it up appropriately when he said, "We are who we are because of our relationships".

It is surprising to me why the importance and the power of business relationships and how to pro-actively manage them is not taught in business schools or courses, or has not been the subject of other self-help areas of study.

Perhaps one of the reasons for this is that, outside of sales, we rarely set goals for our relationships, and therefore have no yardstick with which to measure the progress of strategic relationship development. By setting goals for our relationships, we would be continuously challenging ourselves to improve our relationships and increase our likelihood of success.

It has taken most of my career to understand that business relationships possess an incredible amount of power, directly influencing my success. If used correctly and pro-actively relationships can improve:

- A company's brand
- A company's market position/reputation
- Corporate decision-making
- The quality of the strategic and business plans
- The quality of market research
- The level of corporate exposure to key stakeholders
- The crisis management process.

The right relationships will also reduce business risks by providing a better view and broader perspective on your company, your industry, and any other factors that may impact both your company and industry in the future.

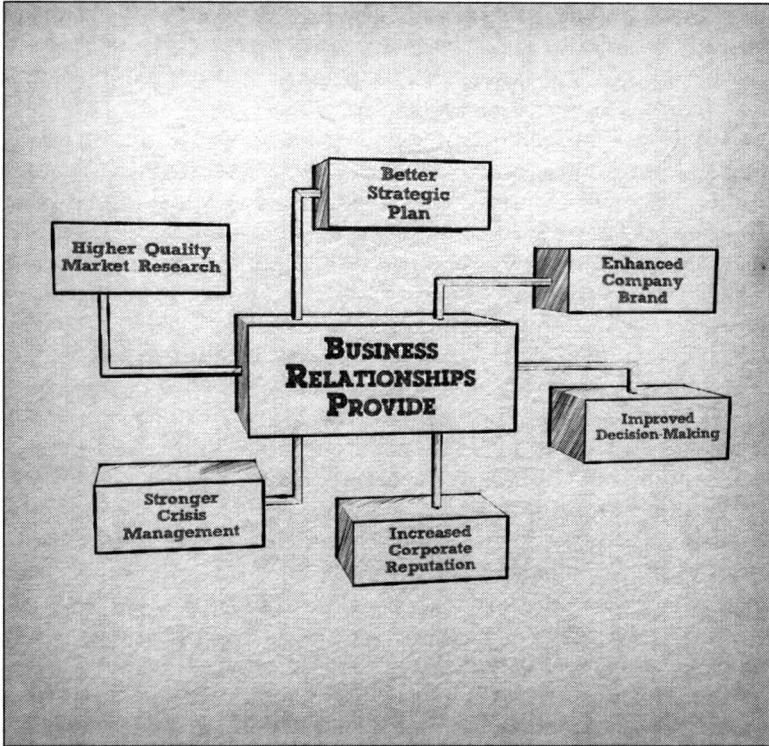

Stakeholder relationships also provide a strong individual benefit. The executive actively building, maintaining and utilizing relationships across their company's key stakeholder groups will reap the following benefits:

- Enhance their personal brand
- Increase their credibility and reputation
- Expand and broaden their personal knowledge base
- Make better, more informed decisions
- Become a better strategic planner
- Expand their career opportunities.

And the news gets even better, because all of these corporate and personal benefits can be achieved with minimal extra effort and minimum additional cost.

3

Now, these are very lofty claims, and one would naturally expect that to achieve such results would require a significant amount of change and money. Again, neither is the case. All of these results can be realized once we look at relationships in the business environment as a competitive advantage.

While this may sound obvious, in reality we do not normally perceive relationships outside of the sales arena in this way. Our relationships have mostly just happened or evolved over time, almost by accident. And, because we already have a number of relationships, we tend to think very little about them or completely take them for granted. What is worse, we can believe we have significant relationships when in truth we do not—*and* we can also mistakenly believe that we have all the relationships we need.

It is easy to understand how we can be quick to ignore relationships as we tend to deal with the urgent matters of the day instead of the important, longer term issues. With the exception of sales, we can quickly become consumed with internal issues.

It is amazing how we can leave the office at the end of the day feeling we have been very busy (which is absolutely the truth) and yet all our activity has been focussed on urgent and internal matters; if we are not mindful, we will find that we have not balanced important, longer-term issues and external contact while meeting immediate demands.

It is not necessary to have a 50/50 split, but it *is* important to have a combination of urgent and important *issues* as well as internal and external *contact*.

So, how do we transform relationships into a competitive advantage that will deliver all the benefits previously stated?

The answer is to turn our relationships from *accidentally* managed to *pro-actively and strategically* managed—and to make sure we have the right level of relationships with the right people at the right time. To make this easier to remember let's call this the "Three Right Rule".

There are three concepts in the Three Right Rule to explore in more detail:

- The first concept is "the right level of relationship" which suggests there is more than one type of relationship. In fact, we will see there are four different levels of business relationships.
- The second concept is to build and maintain the right level of relationship with "the right people". We can-

not have a relationship with everybody. Instead, we need to identify those key individuals within our major stakeholder groups with whom we need to have a high-level relationship. The use of the term "stakeholder" suggests we need to think of relationships in a broader context beyond sales. While the client base is important, it is not the only stakeholder group responsible for our success.

- The third concept is to build the right level of relationship with the right people at "the right time". This part of the Three Right Rule indicates there is a dynamic aspect to relationships that must be considered in order to achieve a sustainable competitive advantage.

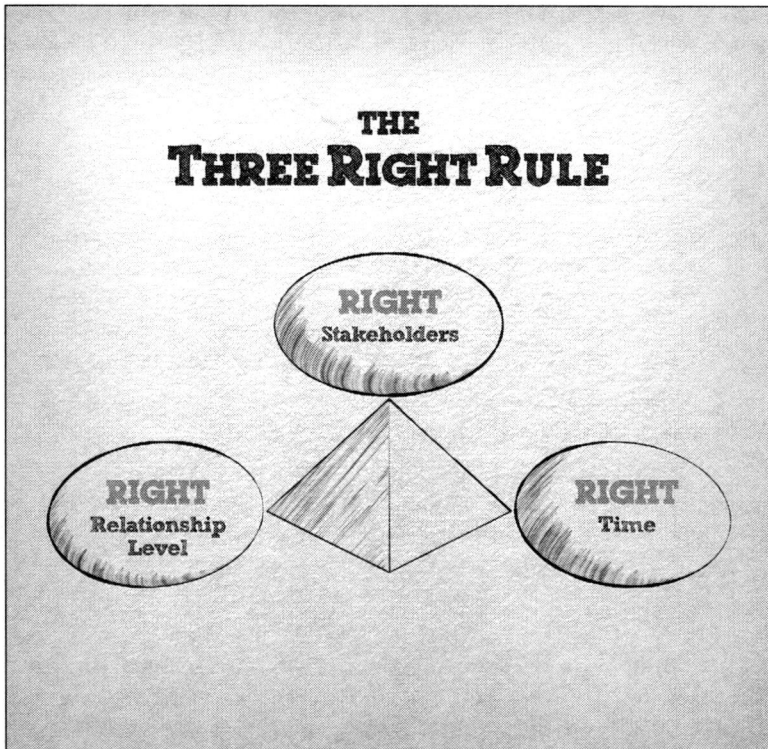

THE

THREE RIGHT RULE

RIGHT
Stakeholders

RIGHT
Relationship
Level

RIGHT
Time

You may be familiar with the phrase "the right place at the right time". This phrase is commonly used to describe how someone, who had just had something good happen to them, was lucky enough because they happened to be in the right place at the right time.

While there is no denying that luck plays a significant role in our lives, I believe we do not have to only rely on luck to be in the right place at the right time when it comes to our relationships.

I believe that, by following pro-active strategic management of our relationships and the Three Right Rule, we can position ourselves to create good results for ourselves and our companies. Additionally, by doing this, *other* people will often recognize that we were in the right place at the right time.

As previously stated, unlocking the power of business relationships does not require significant change or money. It *does* require putting more planning and structure into the relationships we currently have, perhaps using some of these relationships in new ways while developing some new relationships.

All this potential is there for the taking—so let's begin to unleash the competitive advantages of business relationships.

Skill Builder Warm-Up:

- List out on a sheet of paper 20 external relationships you currently have. Make sure they are from 20 different companies/organizations If you are in sale,s make sure at least 10 of the 20 names are from non-direct sales activities. **Keep this list handy as we will refer back to it later.**

- Look back in your diary for the past month and calculate how much of your time has been spent dealing with external relationships.

- If you are in sales, calculate how much of your time was spent on external relationships other than sales calls.

Is it a network or just a bunch of names?

I once attended a conference where a keynote speaker discussed "networking". This speaker was well-acclaimed as he had written several books on the subject. His main thrust was that we are constantly in situations where we can extend our network. At one point during his remarks, he asked the audience how many business cards we collect over the course of any given year. As he went around the room with the number getting higher and higher, something started to dawn on me. He concluded his comments by saying we should be able to gather more than one thousand business cards per year and, of course, hand out the same number of our own business cards.

Upon reflection, I discovered what had bothered me about his premise: a one-time occurrence where business cards are exchanged does not create a meaningful, sustainable relationship and, therefore, does not result in an addition to our network—at least as I define a network. In fact, there is a very good chance the person who collected one thousand business cards over the year would not have come into contact with many of those people again for well over a year—if ever.

Many years ago, my business card holder became so full that I could not possibly fit another card into it. So, I started a purge with the objective of getting rid of the cards where that contact or company was no longer meaningful to me for whatever reason. Not long after I started, I came across a card where I could not remember meeting the individual. As I continued the clean-up exercise, I found, much to my chagrin, a number of names of people that I could no longer recall having ever met. I started to wonder how many of *my* business cards that I had handed out over the years suffered the same fate at the hands of others.

To rectify this, from that day forward, I always wrote on the back of a new business card the date, place and reference note based on the first meeting. I never did this in front of the individual who had just offered up their card to me. I would wait until an appropriate time when I was alone. I felt I had made a major breakthrough in turning a bunch of names on business cards into a real network.

I still use this method; I've learned over the years that it is best to capture the required information on the back of a new business card as soon as possible after the initial meeting. If you wait too long, you run the risk of forgetting some of the information— or in the case where you have collected several business cards at a single event, you risk getting the people and the information confused. Let's say, for example, you attend a conference, and over the course of that event you collect twenty new business cards. If you wait until after you return from the conference to sort the cards and capture the required information on the back of each card, you probably will forget some of the details—or you will confuse the various cards. This becomes even worse if the forgotten information included a "next step" or "follow up" on a specific point. This would mean you missed an opportunity to potentially expand your network in a very meaningful way. If, however, you wrote this information on the back of each card soon after the initial exchange, then your information set is complete, and your next steps or follow-ups can be easily planned.

There are many examples where I developed a long-term senior level relationship with someone, even though the first time we met and exchanged cards I did not consider that type of relationship to be necessary. Circumstances change over time, and so does the need for different levels of relationships. Therefore, it is a good idea to keep all business cards (with corresponding notes on the back) for about a year before purging. Then, if you do need to begin to develop a relationship, you have the ability to easily begin the process.

Many of us today use electronic contact management systems. The same rules apply, because to make an electronic contact management system benefit our relationship management efforts it must allow us to capture the details we have written on the business cards we have collected, and not simply be a repository for name, title, phone number, email address, etc.

If the electronic system does not allow for additional information such as notes and dates to be captured, then a manual system such as the business card holder is also required.

An electronic system that does allow additional information to be recorded is very powerful as it can greatly assist in sorting, scheduling, forward planning, reminders, etc.

Right way, wrong way

There is a right way and a wrong way to exchange business cards. We have already established that you should not write on a person's business card in front of that person. In some cultures this is considered disrespectful. When offered a business card, avoid stuffing it into your pocket without even looking at it. Take a moment or two to give it some respectful attention.

I was at a luncheon one time when a group of individuals from a new start-up vendor arrived. During the pre-lunch reception, these people quickly covered the room, butted into conversations and handed out as many business cards as they possibly could before we were called to lunch. It almost seemed as if they were having a contest amongst themselves as to who could hand out the most cards. I'd be willing to bet that this tactic did not impress many people in the room and that most of their cards that were handed out that day would be in the trash before days' end. To no great surprise, this vendor was out of business in less than a year.

It is best to treat the exchange of business cards with the respect you want to extend to the person with whom you are exchanging cards. When someone hands me their business card I take a moment to study it. I review the name (in case I may have forgotten) as well as the title and where the office is located. This simple action shows that I am taking this opportunity of meeting them seriously, and the quick review allows me to continue the conversation, asking questions about where exactly they are located (especially if they are located in another city) or how long they have been with that company.

I am always amazed at the number of men and women who carry their business cards in their wallets. It's fine to keep a few business cards in your wallet as a last resort, but I do find it odd when I meet someone for the first time in a business setting to see them pull out their wallet, open it up in front of me, and fumble through it for a business card. The card they produce is usually a little dog-eared or smudged, for which they apologize. What a missed opportunity to create a good first impression.

Get a pocket business card holder and use it. I have several card holders that I keep in various portfolios, briefcases, suitcases, and so on, which always prepares me for having a business card to present.

I noticed something else while I was tidying up my card file that day: not all the cards were from the same stakeholder group (for the purposes of this exercise, I defined a stakeholder as any group that can significantly impact your business, or whose business your company can seriously impact). While many of these cards were from clients, there were also cards from industry associations, vendors, regulators, lawyers, accountants, financial community companies and various media. I did not truly recognize the significance of this until later.

A couple of years after my initial business card purge, it came time purge my card file again. I came across the first of many cards where I again could not remember the contact. I thought *I'll just turn the card over and all the information will be on the back to help me remember the individual and the circumstances under which we first met.* All the information was there, and it did allow me to have better

10

recall, but I noticed it had been more than a year since that first meeting and I didn't even know, for example, if that person was still in the same position or if they were even still at the same company. Realizing that I did not have a real relationship with this person, I put that card to the side and all others like it.

As I continued with this exercise, I started to notice a pattern. My card file could be divided into four piles, which I aptly named as follows:

The first pile – the **Initial Contact** level – consisted of those cards where the only contact made had been during the initial exchange of business cards.

The second pile – the **Acquaintance** level – consisted of the group of individuals I saw at conferences, dinners, and receptions. We knew each other's name and would exchange small talk, but we had never had a separate meeting.

The third pile – the **Courting** level – was the group comprising the individuals where I had held one or two meetings—but these meetings were sales meetings or an issue-specific meeting only, and we had not remained in contact since the last meeting.

The last stack of cards – the **Going Steady** level – represented those people I met with on a regular or semi-regular basis; at these meetings, we would discuss broader industry-based issues and future trends.

LEVELS OF RELATIONSHIPS

Going Steady

Courting

Acquaintance

Initial Contact

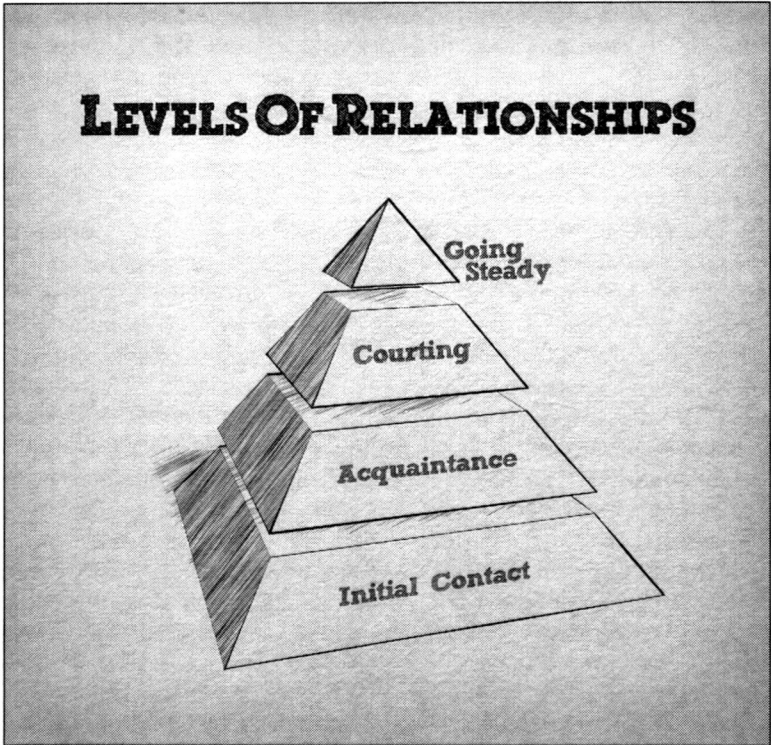

The first pile, the Initial Contact level, had two parts to it. The first was where the initial contact had been made within the last twelve months. The second was where another contact had not occurred for more than twelve months.

Keeping a card where a second contact has not been made for more than a year reminds me of the "**Desperate High School Student Syndrome**". You know the scenario: the high school student, desperate for a date, calls up someone he/she has only met once, briefly, a couple of years ago:

> "Yeah, hi Jim/Judy. You may not remember me, but we met about a year and a half ago at my cousin's wedding. Well, anyway, I was wondering if you were busy on Saturday night?"

I'll bet that Jim/Judy probably, at best, had only a vague recollection of the caller and, not surprisingly, was busy on Saturday night.

The point is that the simple exchange of business cards does not in itself create or expand a network; rather, it opens up the possibility for a relationship to begin. For a business relationship to start to form, the next contact must occur within no more than a twelve-month window. If this does not occur, then it is best treated as a new beginning the next time you are in contact with this individual. To me, a network is the list of people with whom you have some level of ongoing relationship well beyond the initial contact.

I still believe the exchange and collection of business cards is an important exercise—but the cards must be sorted into groups with which you want to have some level of ongoing relationship: Acquaintance, Courting or Going Steady levels and those where you feel an Initial Contact level is sufficient.

In terms of numbers, it's obvious that not all relationships can be at the Going Steady level. In fact, the greatest number of relationships we have will be at the Initial Contact level. Some of these will progress to the Acquaintance state, which in turn will progress to the Courting level. Very few will move to the Going Steady status.

It's not necessary for a relationship to progress through every level. While I think every relationship needs to start at the Initial Contact level, it is possible to move from the Initial Contact level directly to either the Courting or the Going Steady level.

This is why the different types of relationships are referred to as levels instead of phases. The term "phase" suggests an orderly progression from one phase to another, whereas a relationship may remain and be maintained at the same level forever.

A word of caution: it is easy to misread an Acquaintance-level relationship for more than it actually is. There have been occasions where I have reconnected with a person at conferences over the years and therefore had a true Acquaintance-level relationship, only to hear later that they had decided to take their business elsewhere with no notice. This puzzled me, initially, as we had a nice chat at the most recent conference which led me to believe I had a much higher level relationship than was actually the case.

Just because we know someone's name and they know ours and we exchange pleasantries periodically does not put them into a level of relationship with us that would cause them to reach out to us—or, as shown in this example, before making a decision to move their business elsewhere.

The difference between a Courting and Going Steady relationship is that in a Courting relationship there have been a limited number of meetings to date, and the interaction between you and your contact is specific-issue-based, such as a sales call. In a true Going Steady relationship, you would interact with your contact a number of times over the course of any given year, and would seek their input and advice on various broader-based business issues and trends. These are the people with whom you have an on-going business relationship at the highest level.

Relationships are assets

I personally view relationships at the Going Steady level as part of a company's assets. Granted, they may be "soft" assets as compared to plant, equipment, etc. but they play an important role in the continued success of a company.

If the "hard" assets of a company such as plant, equipment, etc. are either not the right assets for the job or are not used and maintained properly, then the overall success of the company is limited. If, however, these hard assets are selected, used and maintained properly, the company will likely flourish.

Relationships (and other soft assets) can provide the same positive result for the company if the right relationships are formed, utilized and maintained.

I am continually amazed at the number of people who just don't get it. These are smart, accomplished people who excel in every other aspect of their jobs *except* in building the right relationships (at the right level) with the right people at the right time.

These people do have relationships at various levels with lots of people, but the relationships have happened, for the most part, by accident. Imagine the power if these relationships were strategically planned in such a way as to maximize the benefit to your company.

While the initial meeting between you and a new contact is important, it is the ongoing relationship you form with some of these individuals that will provide you with long-term success. It is the Going Steady relationship, for example, that will keep the doors open for discussion, determine when and how quickly your call will be taken or returned, provide the heads-up or the second chance, give the honest feedback and, in the case of with a client, create opportunities to work with you through issues instead of voting with their feet and taking their business elsewhere without any notice.

One of the things I enjoy most about these Going Steady relationships is the ability to discuss new challenges facing our company or facing the member of a particular stakeholder group with whom I am meeting. These relationships also allow for the identification, verification or change in existing trends within a particular industry that might affect our business. I can use this information in our decision-making and during our strategic planning process.

These relationships can also be of particular benefit when you are considering a move into a new product line or a new market.

Is an Advisory Committee a replacement for Going Steady relationships?

It is important to recognize and understand the differences between Going Steady relationships and Advisory Committees.

An advisory committee usually consists of a fixed set of participants that meet as a group on a semi-regular basis. They may or may not include members from various key stakeholder groups and, if they do include members from across a number of stakeholder groups, it is normally only one member per stakeholder group. Because advisory committees meet in groups, the topics covered may be restricted, or the participation by the members guarded.

Going Steady relationships need to cover all key stakeholder groups, and number in excess of what you would find in an advisory committee. This relationship level covers more than one representative per key stakeholder group; the meetings are one-on-one, so the topics are not restricted, and dialogue is not guarded.

A Going Steady relationship is not mentoring

It is important not to confuse the Going Steady level of relationship with Mentoring.

You may have many Going Steady relationships in place at the same time. In comparison, a person usually only has one mentor at any given time. In fact, it is common for a person to never have a mentor at any time during their entire career.

I have been fortunate to have had two mentors over my career. One of the significant benefits from my mentee experience was how to problem solve. I could either talk it out with my mentor, or I could ask myself, "*What would my mentor do in this situation, and how would they approach this problem?*"

I have volunteered in a mentoring program for business students at the University of Toronto at Scarborough for several years. Each year, we were assigned a student to mentor for the entire school year. While I benefited from participating in this program, the real focus of the program was, of course, the student.

As a mentor, our objective was to help develop the knowledge and skill levels of the students based on our practical business and management experience. In short, we wanted to better prepare them for a career in business.

In a Going Steady relationship, we are not seeking career guidance, personal advice, or to model our decision-making, problem solving approach to that of our Going Steady colleague.

A Going Steady relationship (as well as Initial Contact, Acquaintance, and Courting relationships) is on an equal peer-to-peer basis.

A Going Steady relationship is not the same as a Business Confidant

A business confidant is someone we have an extreme level of trust and would share information, emotions and feelings that we would not share with anyone else. As with mentors, we would probably have only one confidant at a time, and for many of us, we may never have anyone who would be considered a business confidant.

Similar to mentor relationships, in a business confidant relationship we do not come to the table as equals unless our business confidant equally shares information, emotions and feelings with us. Usually, a business confidant relationship is single-sided with one person doing the majority of sharing and the other providing comment, advice and counsel.

While there are similarities between a mentor and a business confidant, the main difference is that in a mentor relationship we are seeking a role model, and in a business confidant relationship we are not.

In a business confidant relationship, we are also seeking personal advice and guidance which again makes this type of relationship quite different from a Going Steady relationship.

The whole truth and nothing but the truth

Have you ever noticed that in some discussions, you are told certain things only to find out later that you were only being told what was believed to be what you wanted to hear? Or that the other person was just being polite and did not want to tell you their real thoughts on a particular matter? The higher you go in the relationship spectrum (from Initial Contact to Going Steady), the higher the level of trust develops between you and your colleague. This trust will ensure you receive the real thoughts and feelings from these individuals even if it is not exactly what you expected or wanted to hear. This greater level of trust is essential if we are to use this information in strategic planning, decision-making and product development.

When selecting a specific stakeholder with whom you want to build a Going Steady relationship, it is always beneficial to choose a person who will give you open, honest and direct comment or feedback. It is important to remember that you want a diversity of opinion, perspective and interpretation from your relationships, so resist the urge to only develop relationships with people that are like-minded to you.

As you would already have a lower-level relationship with these individuals, it should not be that difficult to make a choice.

TRUST VARIES DIRECTLY WITH LEVEL OF RELATIONSHIP

High

TRUST

Low

Initial Contact   Going Steady

RELATIONSHIP LEVEL

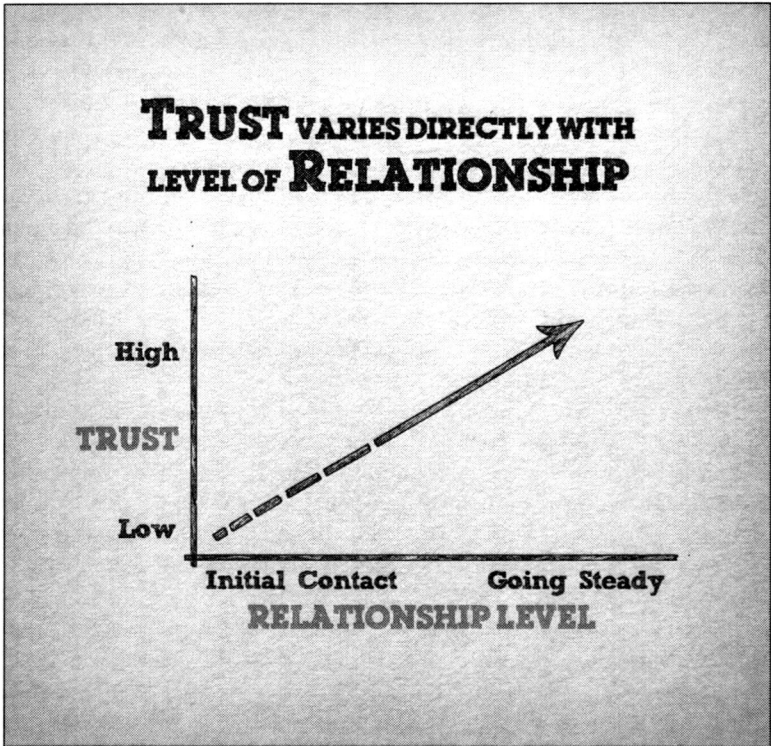

We have already seen that you cannot have the same number of Acquaintance, Courting or Going Steady relationships as you do initial meetings where you exchange business cards. The presenter at that conference I mentioned at the beginning of this chapter suggested we should collect one thousand business cards per year—but it is not possible to extent your number of Acquaintance, Courting or Going Steady relationships by one thousand per year while keeping them all active and meaningful.

I also believe the number of relationships that can be maintained at any given time varies by individual because of personality, energy, location, and other possible factors. The important thing is for us to determine what is the right number of relationships we can manage and to focus our attention on those relationships.

So, when is a network really a network? The answer is this: when it is comprised of meaningful, sustainable relationships. Until then, it is simply a lot of names on either a bunch of business cards or within an electronic file.

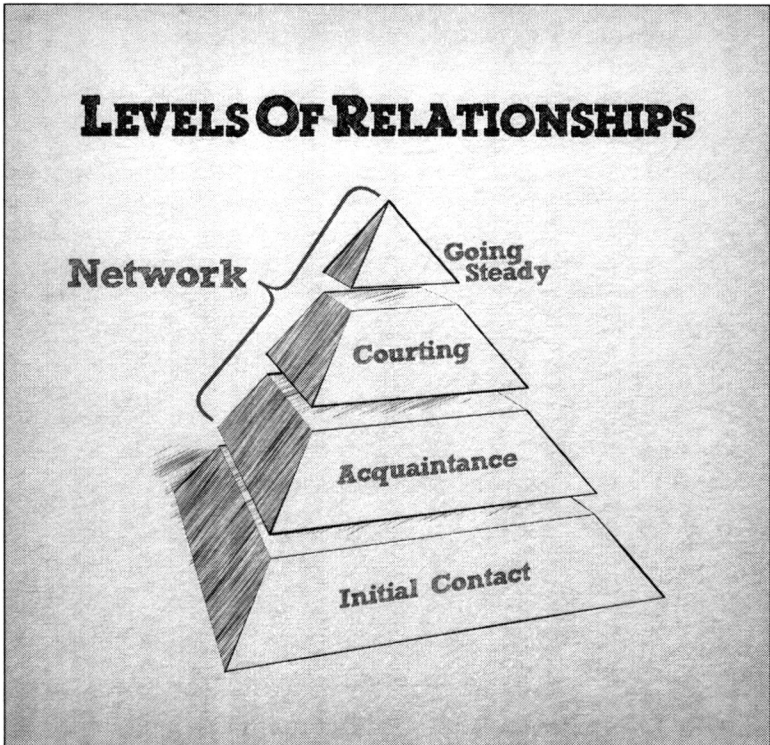

Skill Builder Warm Up:

Take the list of 20 names you identified in the previous Warm Up, and, by being brutally honest with yourself, record your current level of relationship for each one:

- **Initial Contact** – only the exchange of business cards has occurred with no other contact. Subdivide this group into two subsets. The subset is where initial contact has occurred within the previous twelve months, and the remainder is where the initial contact happened more than twelve months ago.

- **Acquaintance** – there is face/name/company recognition

and typically you come into contact with these people at conferences, group breakfasts/luncheons/dinners/receptions.

- **Courting** – you have met with the contact once or twice since the original exchange of business cards and these meetings were to discuss specific topics.
- **Going Steady** – you meet with the individual on a regular or semi-regular basis and discuss broader issues.

The next task is to look at each of these names and determine if your current level of relationship is the right category of relationship needed, given their level of importance to your company.

A key point to remember with the names in the Initial Contact group, especially where a second contact has not been made in over a year, is that it is rarely too late to start building a relationship. When this occurs, it probably does require you to initiate the next contact and to have a valid reason for doing so.

Next, identify all the stakeholder groups for your company and identify any stakeholder groups where you currently do not have at least a Courting or Going Steady relationship.

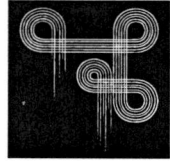

You Need a Relationship
before you need
a Relationship

Through all the learning and experience I have gathered in the area of business relationships, the most important lesson I have learned is that, when facing a serious crisis, challenge or priority, it is better to have the right relationship (right level of relationship with the right person at the right time) already in place than to have an inadequate relationship in place—or, even worse, no relationship at all with the people with whom you now have to start dealing.

With the right relationship in place you are better able to hit the ground running to effectively deal with your crisis, challenge or priority; you will stand a better chance for a more positive outcome than when no pre-existing relationship is in place.

In many ways a relationship is like a bank account. You would not consider going into a bank and asking for money from an account you did not have with that bank. A relationship works in much the same way.

Let's look at this closer by way of an example of a scenario that we would prefer not to happen:

We have all probably experienced a variation on the following: a serious problem arises with one of your large clients that threatens your business. Your sales department asks for help as the magnitude of this problem is beyond the level of their contact within the client's organization. Then it hits you like a sharp pain between your eyes: neither you nor anyone at your company has a relationship with anyone at the client company at the level with whom you now need to communicate. You need to contact the client, but you do not have a foundation established through an existing senior level relationship to make the call.

Without a pre-existing relationship, that call goes something like this

> "Hello, we have not had the opportunity to meet yet but I wanted to contact you directly and apologize for the issue we caused you today. Your business is very important to us and I want to assure you we are taking this matter very seriously..."

But, in the absence of a pre-existing relationship, what the person on the other end of the phone actually heard was:

> "Hello, I've not contacted you previously, because neither you nor your business is important enough to us—but now that we have screwed up, I have to make this call and beg for forgiveness..."

Do you think the person on the other end of the phone feels as though their business has been taken for granted? Ouch! When this happens it actually feels like *two* mistakes have occurred. The first mistake is that there was no relationship established, and the second error lies within the actual problem that the client is now experiencing.

Let's be clear: Making the call and doing everything you can to correct or salvage the situation even though you do not have an existing relationship is better than *not* making the call at all.

Lesson learned: You need to build a meaningful, sustainable ongoing relationship before you have to call on that relationship to deal with a significant business issue or further a business cause. Without the right relationship already in place, you are making it extremely easy for a client to vote with their feet and simply take their business elsewhere.

And, as we all know, once a client has made the decision to go to the competition, the likelihood of reversing that decision and regaining that business in the short-term is remote.

A true-life example of this happened to me several years ago when I was in one of our branch offices and had arranged a dinner with a senior contact of a major client. I chose to have dinner with this contact as he was also recognized as a leader both within his industry and his profession. The dinner was not a sales call. Instead, it was a meeting where we discussed trends and challenges within both his industry and profession, and how we saw both evolving over time.

Well, the very next day we made a significant error on this client's file. It quickly became apparent that this issue could not be resolved at the sales level and, in fact, my dinner guest from the night before called me directly. I will never know, had I not had an existing high level relationship that I had been nurturing the night before, if he would have ever made the call. The story had a happy ending as we retained the client—but this certainly showed me the power and importance of a real business relationship.

Another example with a not-so-happy outcome occurred a few years later when we committed an error with a large client. While it is not possible to have a relationship at the Courting or Going Steady level with every client, we should have had one at a senior level with this important client. Despite a lot of scrambling and best efforts, we were unable to retain the account.

Another example when I was on the other side of the table; this happened shortly after I joined an organization in a senior management role. Our office lease was coming up for renewal within seventeen months of my start date. Months went by, and the existing landlord made no attempt to reach out to us. They were unaware that a new senior person had started who was responsible for all lease agreements. Meanwhile, we were approached by several commercial real estate agents and began looking at alternative office locations.

Finally, I contacted our existing landlord and kick-started discussions. They scrambled to try and catch up to where we were in the process, but found it hard as they had not built any relationship with me prior to jumping directly into an office lease renewal negotiation.

The end result? We relocated to another office location with a new landlord.

Let's move beyond the client realm with another example: A regulator of your industry has announced a review of the regulations that could have a serious effect on your business. You feel that sharp pain between your eyes returning as you realize you have no relationship with the regulator and had no idea that the regulations affecting your business were even being considered for a review. In fact, you have always avoided them as you consider them a necessary evil.

Sometimes you need to build and maintain relationships with stakeholder groups (other than clients) with whom you would otherwise not choose to associate.

Unfortunately, most of us learn the lesson of needing to have a relationship in place before we need to draw on that relationship the hard way—during a crisis.

The most vivid example of the best way to prepare for a potential crisis comes from a colleague in the transportation industry:

A few years ago, we were discussing travel schedules and he outlined all the cities across Canada he would visit during a two-to-three-year period. There were the usual big city names but also a surprising number of smaller cities.

He wasn't in sales, so I asked why he visited so many smaller cities.

His reply was that, despite his company's excellent record, at some point in the future it might be involved in a crisis in a particular part of the country that would affect one of these cities. If that were to happen, the company would need strong, established, high-level relationships with key stakeholders from these cities already in place when they launched their crisis management plan.

Otherwise, the company would be dealing with a bunch of unknown stakeholders which would severely hamper and possibly impede their crisis management efforts and potentially damage their reputation.

Take the offense

Up until now we have been examining the need to have established, pre-existing relationships for defensive reasons. There is also the need to have established, pre-existing relationships for offensive reasons.

Examples include: planning for a new product, researching a new competitive advantage, or pro-active positioning for seeking a regulatory change.

Again, be very careful, as one of the greatest delusions we have as business people is to believe we have more true ongoing relationships at the Courting or Going Steady level than we actually do. For example, we mistakenly believe someone we only see at the occasional conference or reception is at a senior-relationship level when in actual fact we really only have an Acquaintance-level relationship. Usually we discover the true level of relationship only when a crisis or significant challenge occurs with their organization and we do not have the benefit of a senior-level relationship to draw on. This rarely works to our advantage, and while a relationship at the Acquaintance level is better than nothing, it does not carry the same value or weight as that of a Going Steady relationship.

Given the worldwide recession of 2008/2009 (a crisis situation for many companies), I wonder: How many people learned the hard way that you need a relationship in place before you need to draw on that relationship?

I think there is an aspect of human nature that, until recognized, works against us when developing relationships at the right level with the right people.

The natural tendency is to develop a relationship at the Going Steady level with the people we like and whose companionship we enjoy. We can have many relationships of this type and, therefore, can easily fool ourselves into thinking we have our relationship needs covered. A tell-tale sign of this behaviour is when one of these individuals leaves their position. Do we begin to build a new relationship with their replacement? Or do we wait to see where our contact surfaces and continue the ongoing relationship with them instead?

Assuming the organization is one we should have a Going Steady relationship at a senior staff level, once the departure is known we should immediately begin to build a new relationship with their replacement. We should progress this new relationship as quickly as possible and take it to at least the Courting level—and eventually to the Going Steady level.

At one time I had built a Going Steady relationship with a senior executive at a regulator. This relationship served us well. Then that contact left the regulator, and while we should have built a senior-level relationship with their replacement, we did not. As a result, our ability to have our voice heard and ideas considered by this regulator diminished greatly, as did our awareness of future areas of focus of the regulator.

It is important to begin this process of forming a new relationship as soon as possible because, until you do, despite the strength of your relationship with the previous incumbent, you are at risk with this organization, especially if they are a client.

So, with whom do you need to have relationships? This is an important question; the answer is really with anyone that could have a major impact on your business.

This list includes key clients (especially in business-to-business). But relationships are needed with *all* other key stakeholder groups, such as suppliers, bankers, lawyers, regulatory bodies, shareholders, industry associations, analysts, media, etc. No doubt you have relationships with people within some of these groups right now. The question is, do you have a relationship at the right level with everyone with whom you need to have a relationship, and are you maintaining those relationships?

Compiling a list of the relationships you need can be quite daunting. And of course, the list keeps changing and expanding frequently as new players emerge, or people with whom you have built a relationship change positions, retire or leave the industry.

The currency of relationships is important in order to avoid the situation where you need to draw on your relationship account, only then to find out the person with whom you had the relationship is no longer with the company—or that they are still at the same company but in a different capacity.

One time we heard that a client was moving to a competitor. I was surprised by this as I thought I had a Going Steady relationship built with an executive at that firm. I was even more surprised to learn that the executive I thought I had a Going Steady relationship with had changed jobs within the company and was now in another department. In hindsight, I realized it had been well over a year since my last contact with this person, so my Going Steady relationship had eroded. I had been taking the relationship for granted, had not been paying enough attention to it and, as a result, paid a significant price.

Remember the four categories into which we divided our business cards? Initial Contact, Acquaintance, Courting and Going Steady. After looking at the issue just discussed, it is easy to see that, the higher the level of relationship, the greater the chance of success in dealing with an issue.

The challenge is to have the right relationship with the right number of people at the right time across all stakeholder categories—remember the Three Right Rule.

Your list of target relationships may seem longer than you can handle on an on-going basis. The good news is that you don't have to manage all these by yourself; you can share the task with your colleagues.

This makes a lot of sense, because you shouldn't have one person in your company with all the relationships with your key stakeholders. Having only one person at a company with all the key stakeholder relationships is called the "Sole Face" syndrome. That's a significant risk if that person leaves.

You should vary the responsibilities for relationships with your executive group across each stakeholder segment, thus eliminating this risk.

This is similar to a rule of marketing that says you should avoid having a brand associated with one person only. The reason is simple: If the brand is built around one person and that person leaves, then the brand suffers as a result. Relationships are too important to the success of your company to be centred on one person only.

That is not to say that having only one person within a company with all the relationships at the Going Steady level is bad. It is certainly better than having no one managing relationships at all.

There's another benefit to spreading the relationship wealth amongst a group of your colleagues: If only one person is providing feedback from their relationships, then it is subject to their interpretations, perspectives and biases. But if feedback is given by a group of executives for a particular stakeholder segment then this risk is reduced and decision-making improves.

What we are talking about is creating a strategic relationship program for your company consisting of relationships at the Going Steady level that involves your peers from within your firm and covers all your stakeholder groups.

It's also important to build relationships with more than one stakeholder representative within any one constituency group. This ensures you gain a sense of the variation of thought and perspective on a particular topic and eliminates the possibility of using input from a single stakeholder. This is key as a single representative may be an outlier because of their particular interpretations, perspectives or biases from the rest of that stakeholder segment.

This "Relationship Layering" means that, with any one major stakeholder entity, there will be at least two relationships maintained. This is necessary to validate the information that is being obtained from that particular stakeholder representative. Again, this works best if at least two executives from your company develop and maintain the relationships within a single stakeholder group.

Another benefit of Relationship Layering is that it gives the ability to match the right personalities between your stakeholders and your executives.

We have all experienced the situation where, despite our best efforts and for whatever reason, we just did not hit it off with the other person. The personality mix was just not right.

A real-life example of this happened in our company a few years ago involving an important client in our Montreal office. This client could not connect with any of our local sales staff, including the VP of sales for that region. After trying various approaches, we found the right staff member from another office to connect with this particular client; this staff member successfully managed the relationship and the account.

If one stakeholder is not connecting with one of your executives, or if one of your executives does not like dealing with a certain stakeholder, relationship layering allows you to simply change to another executive until you find the right match.

It is important to ensure, to the greatest extent possible, the comfort level of your executives with the list of stakeholders they are responsible for managing as a senior relationship. Otherwise, it is quite easy for an executive to become apprehensive in participating in a stakeholder relationship program if he/she does not like some of the stakeholders on their list. Be aware, they may not tell you that directly—instead, it may come out in comments such as "I've been too busy" if asked why they have not been meeting and advancing their relationships with that particular stakeholder. It is essential to have the right level of relationship—even with the stakeholders that have difficult personalities.

Stakeholder relationship succession planning

We watched a significant stakeholder of ours go through a very unfortunate event: This stakeholder had an executive who was expert at stakeholder relationships. The problem arose when this person announced their retirement and, while they had a succession plan in place, it did not include dealing with the senior relationships (Courting and Going Steady) that this executive had established over the years.

When this executive retired, all these relationships vanished. What a waste! By being proactive on the management of senior relationships from a corporate level, this could have easily been avoided.

All that was required was some lead time for other executives to create and build those relationships. This assumes the executive's departure was known ahead of time. If not, then new relationships should be established as soon as possible following the departure.

Skill Builder Warm Up:

At the end of the previous chapter we identified all the stakeholder groups with whom your company should have senior relationships.

- Either on your own, or working with a group of colleagues, or with the involvement of all your senior executives, under each constituency, list the appropriate names from the card-sorting exercise. List any additional names which should be included but for whom you do not have an existing relationship.

- Divide the list of target stakeholders with whom you or your fellow executives currently do not have a relationship amongst the participating executive group. Again, make sure no one executive has all the relationship responsibility with a single stakeholder segment.

- The number of target stakeholders may be too large for the group of executives involved. If that is the case, then make the tough decisions and prioritize the stakeholder list so a realistic number is achieved. If you are doing this on your own, then prioritizing is extremely important in order for you to achieve a workable number of senior relationships.

It is important to get the right stakeholder-to-executive ratio—otherwise, meaningful and sustainable relationships will not be developed, and the program will suffer. And if the program suffers, the benefits to your company will not be fully realized, and you will limit your company's success.

It is better to have a smaller number of true relationships than a large number of half-baked relationships.

29

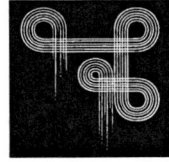

Not Every Relationship
is Created Equal

Another way to maximize your effectiveness in dealing with the number of people with whom you need to maintain a Going Steady relationship is to leverage the "Connected People". The Connected People are the ones who actively maintain a significant network of their own. They typically are well-known and respected within their constituency and are always networking. They have the classic "people person" personality.

Because of their vast network of relationships, they can be a great source of information since they have perspectives from across their extensive network.

You will want to verify the input you receive from Connected People with others in the various stakeholder groups to identify and eliminate any biases or misinterpretations the Connected People may have.

Making sure that the Connected People are prime contacts in your network results in a leveraging effect; they will often spread the news about you and your company while *they* are networking.

This acts as a great reinforcement of the message you are communicating with your relationship-building activities since the connected people will repeat your key message throughout their own vast networks. This repetition of your message by the Connected People allows for greater retention of your key messages by those on the receiving end.

Another potential benefit of including the Connected People in *your* network is that they may also include you in *their* network. It is quite common for Connected People to host networking events throughout the year. By being a part of their network, you will get invited to their networking functions, giving you the opportunity to expand your existing network by both meeting new potential members and furthering any of your existing relationships with existing stakeholder members who are also attending these functions.

Do not be afraid to utilize a Connected Person's network, as Connected People can always provide you with an introduction to new contacts.

Individuals who also provide great leverage are those who represent more than one stakeholder group. They could be a client who is a leader of an important industry association, or an executive within an industry association who also might sit on a regulatory advisory committee. I think of people in this category whenever I hear of an individual described as one who "wears many hats".

These are "Multi-Stakeholder" individuals who allow you to gain perspectives from each stakeholder group in a single meeting. They also help spread your key messages amongst the groups in which they are active.

It is easy to see how Multi-Stakeholders provide substantial efficiency and benefit to our Senior Strategic Relationship program.

Several years ago, our sales group was prospecting a company that had switched to a competitor two years earlier. Since the switch, there had been a change in personnel, and the new senior decision-maker was quickly being recognized as an industry leader, and was becoming very involved in an important industry association.

None of us knew this person. So, while our sales team continued discussions with the appropriate level within this prospect, another senior executive and myself started building a relationship with the new decision-maker.

The relationship flourished over the years; not only did we win the account back—the new relationship provided valuable insight into the industry association where this person was actively moving into a senior leadership role. Additionally, we could soon see that, within this industry segment, our company was being recognized at a higher level of credibility and leadership. This was no doubt due to this important individual helping spread the word.

When this same individual began planning for their retirement, we were able to implement a good transition plan in order to cultivate a Going Steady relationship built with their successor *before* the effective date of the previous contact's retirement.

Seek out the Spokesperson

A third group of unique people with whom we need to build ongoing relationships is the "Spokesperson" group. This is the group of individuals you will see most often quoted in both traditional and social media regarding matters affecting your industry or the industries your company serves. A person becomes a spokesperson in one of two ways: either the media search them out (usually because of their position, expertise or reputation) or a person will let the media know they are available to comment on a given range of topics. Once the media identify an industry expert (one of these Spokespeople) they tend to repeatedly use that source over time.

A variation on the second way a person becomes a Spokesperson is when they become active in social networking, regularly commenting on industry affairs and issues. They do this either through their own social networking sites, by actively contributing on other sites, or both.

Caution: The social networking world does not necessarily behave in the same way as traditional media. You should become familiar with the social networking space and the particular relevant sites or groups before embarking on a relationship-building program in this arena.

Sometimes it takes an event to identify the Spokespeople for the various industry sectors.

My own learning curve in this area happened a number of years ago at the time our company was involved in a transaction that received a lot of attention in the media—most of which was not positive. I quickly identified the Spokespeople the media sought out for comment. One was from our client/prospect stakeholder group, the other from one of the regulatory bodies. These Spokespeople did not contact either me or my company ahead of their interview with the media to ascertain our perspective on the transaction. Why would they? At the time, I only had an Acquaintance-level relationship with both of them.

Based on that experience, I immediately put these two people on my target list for a stronger relationship, and over the course of the next couple of years I moved my relationship level with one of these individuals to the Going Steady status. Once I reached the Going Steady level, I noticed a change in behaviour. The next time a potentially contentious issue came forward that involved our firm, the Spokesperson personally called me to discuss it before making any public comment.

Now, does the simple fact that you have a senior ongoing relationship with a Spokesperson mean there will always be a positive outcome? Of course not. But it *does* substantially improve your chances of either diffusing an issue before it appears in the media, or at the very least, ensuring that your side of the story is told and hopefully understood.

To finish the story: the other Spokesperson left the industry soon after this issue was resolved and was no longer in a Spokesperson role or a key stakeholder. Had that person stayed in their position and continued to act as a Spokesperson I would have built a stronger, more senior relationship with them.

It goes without saying that someone from your own company should be a Spokesperson for your industry. That person should build their relationships with the media (daily, trade publications and social media) so they will be contacted by the media for comment and/or response. The last thing you want to read is a news story about your industry where your company is not even referenced and, even worse, your competitor has been quoted in the article or interview.

If this happens, it means that your competition has a higher-level relationship with the media and the various Spokespeople than you do at that particular point in time. The good news is that by building stronger relationships with the media and these Spokespeople, you will now have a way to counteract your competitor's advantage.

It is not out of the question for a person to be a Connected Person, Multi-Stakeholder and a Spokesperson—or any two of the three.

An example of this is a Connected Person who is the voluntary Chairperson of an industry association and also, because of their voluntary Chairperson role, a Spokesperson.

Including this person in your ongoing relationship network brings a significant efficiency to your relationship-building efforts.

Skill Builder Warm Up:

We now see that not everyone on our relationship list is created equal, so it is important to ensure that the names of the Connected People, the Multi-Stakeholder and the Spokesperson individuals are identified across all stakeholder groups and included in this exercise. Remember, these individuals provide great leverage of your time.

The same rules apply to this group as to the other names on your relationship list. Ensure the Connected People, the Multi-Stakeholder and Spokesperson names are divided up and spread across all your executives involved with this program.

If you are not quite ready to involve other senior executives, then complete this exercise based on your network of relationships; determine where you need to expand your network either within an existing stakeholder group or a new stakeholder group where you currently have no relationships.

Making Deposits to Your Relationship Accounts

It astounds me the number of times at executive meetings or strategic planning sessions where decisions are made where none or few of the executives have spoken to their constituencies on the matter on which the decision is being taken.

I call this "Input Isolation". In these situations, we are either making decisions in a vacuum without the benefit of any external knowledge, or we are relying solely on the input from others—such as sales or marketing representatives—to tell us what our client base is thinking on any given issue. Additionally, we lack input from any other stakeholder group beyond our client base. The question is, as executives, have we isolated ourselves from our constituents relying, at best, on feedback from others which may or may not be filtered or biased?

Input Isolation is dangerous because it is a natural human tendency to think we know what's best for others, and to draw conclusions about what other groups think about certain situations or issues without taking the time to actually consult any of them. We often do this without even realizing we are making and communicating these assumptions as if they are undisputed facts; if challenged, we will often defend these assumptions with great vigour.

Time and time again, I have seen market research and perception studies that show the expectations of management were not completely correct when matched against actual survey results from a particular stakeholder group.

There is also a variation of Input Isolation: Someone hears a single comment from a client or a member of some other stakeholder organization, but communicates this as the position of the *entire* client base or stakeholder group where the comment originated.

This is dangerous—what if that one comment does not represent the attitudes of the majority of a group? What if that group is thinking the exact opposite or something significantly different? How does one determine the true nature of comments when they are communicated during an executive meeting or strategic planning session?

Imagine how much more successful your executive meetings, decision-making and strategic planning sessions would be if your entire executive group has been discussing, through ongoing relationships with key constituency members at the Going Steady level, the challenges, trends and new developments that may affect your company's future.

How much more effective would your SWOT analysis (Strengths, Weaknesses, Opportunities and Threats) and your PEST analysis (Political, Economic, Societal and Technological) be with external input from all your stakeholder groups?

A real-life example of this happened to me a few years ago. I had developed a Going Steady relationship with the President of a European affiliate.

In a discussion about strategy it became apparent that the affiliate had developed a technical solution that provided greater operational efficiency and improved customer service.

Because of our Going Steady relationship, the President of the affiliate was eager to share their technology with us; they arranged for our respective information technology staff to meet and discuss the software they had developed.

I recall that at a meeting, one of their Information Technology staff members, who had just been brought into the meeting, was hesitant to discuss their work. Their President, with whom I had the Going Steady relationship, assured his staff member that it was permissible to participate fully in the discussion.

This exchange allowed us to address a weakness we had identified in our own SWOT analysis more quickly than we had previously thought possible.

The way to avoid Input Isolation is to first recognize that it exists, and then build a strategic relationship program utilizing your executive group that covers all your key stakeholders.

Eye on the ball

Another tendency to avoid is hitting a "Relationship Plateau". As we all have a number of existing relationships in place, it is easy to be lulled into a false sense of security and think we have all the relationships we need. We take our eye off the relationship ball.

We stop (or extremely reduce) our relationship activity by slowing the number of interactions with our existing senior relationships and/or we stop developing new relationships at the Courting and Going Steady levels.

Unfortunately, it usually takes a crisis or major event to make us realize we have hit a relationship plateau and that we must restart our proactive relationship management efforts.

One of the best ways to avoid getting stuck in a relationship plateau is to annually review the relationships you have and identify the new senior relationships you need. The best way to schedule this annual review is to include it as part of your strategic planning/review or, if you are not doing annual strategic planning, to include it alongside your business planning efforts as part of your annual budgeting process.

In the previous chapter I referred to the similarities between relationships and bank accounts. Another way relationships are similar to bank accounts is that they both need continuing deposits in order to grow.

Each time we make meaningful contact with a person we are, in a sense, making a deposit into our relationship account with that person. Just as there are several ways to make a deposit into our bank accounts there are also several ways to make deposits into our relationship accounts. A meaningful deposit into your relationship account can be in any form of personal communication, such as email, phone calls, text messages and, of course, in person. These deposits must be made periodically in order for our account balance to grow—and those deposits need to be made a bit more frequently at the start of a new relationship. Once a relationship is established and reaches the Going Steady level, the deposits do not have to be made as often.

My typical approach to begin to develop a Going Steady relationship is to initiate an in-person, informal meeting over breakfast, lunch or coffee. It is most effective to meet in a neutral location as it eliminates any sense of a home court advantage. Remember, we want the conversation to be open and frank. This can only happen if both you and your stakeholder are relaxed. I find it best to put the person I want to build a relationship with at ease immediately by reinforcing the fact that there is no agenda—it is just a chance for each of us to get to know each other a little better and discuss industry issues, challenges and trends. This usually has a great calming effect on the participant as it eliminates any concerns that you are going to try and sell them something or re-negotiate a contract. By restating the "no agenda" rule at the start of the meeting, my guest quickly becomes quite open in their conversation, letting down any guard they might have come with to this first meeting.

I also believe that asking someone for their opinion on any topic is a great show of respect for that individual; this act demonstrated over a period of time has a magical impact on building a strong and lasting relationship. When one shows respect, quite often one gains respect in return.

Being on time shows respect

Speaking of respect, simply being on time for a meeting or appointment is one of the first indications you can give of having respect for the colleague with whom you are meeting.

Being on time is almost completely within our control, except in those very few times of unavoidable delays, such as getting a flat tire. You notice I did not say "traffic" or "parking" as I believe that we should be able to allow enough time to arrive on time.

Being late for a meeting indicates one of two things: We are either poor time managers or the meeting was not that important to us, so showing up late was okay. The latter is cause for concern since it conveys a lack of respect for those people with whom you are meeting.

If you are going to be late, then call, text or email to let your colleague know you will not be there on time. This applies to meetings, conference calls, pre-scheduled phone calls, etc. Simply do not make being late become a habit.

Caution

It seems to be in vogue to tell each other how busy we are. It's almost like we wear how busy we are as some kind of badge of honour; be very careful with using the *I'm too busy* excuse for being late, because it can be interpreted as an insult to whomever you are meeting.

We are *all* very busy; using the *I'm too busy* excuse for being late implies that you believe that you are busier than the individual you are meeting with, because *they* made the meeting on time.

In their mind, if you think you are busier than they are, then maybe you also think you are more important than they are.

These are perceptions you do not need to create, and they certainly do not help develop a relationship.

The excuse for being late because you are just too busy is *not* acceptable, since the real solution is to simply book the meeting for another time.

Pre-Work is important

Before I invite anyone to one of these meetings, I first identify any strategic issues and trends in which I want to gain further insight and perspective. I also identify which key stakeholder groups may have a relevant perspective on a particular issue or trend. For example, I may want to gain greater understanding on a specific issue from the perspective of a client, a regulator, a consultant or academic. I then formulate the series of questions I will ask using various questioning techniques.

Developing a series of questions ahead of time on the topics I want to discuss is important as it has been my experience that simply asking "What's new?" or "How's it going?" very rarely generates a meaningful response at the start of a conversation.

My preparation allows me to guide our conversation and focus our discussion. It also allows me to pay more attention to listening to responses rather than trying to think of another question or comment while my guest is speaking—possibly missing an important comment.

However, I always include an open-ended question toward the end of our meeting to identify any new trends or challenges the stakeholder is facing or sees on the horizon that has not yet hit my radar. If I identify a new trend or challenge, I do some research within our own company and, if warranted, include this as a new topic of conversation in my future relationship-building meetings.

Next, in my pre-meeting preparation, I determine the key messages I want to communicate about my company.

I find it most effective to only have two or three key messages at most; any more than three key messages diminishes the likelihood of your contact retaining them.

These key messages should be developed for use by your entire company, which ensures consistency and priority.

It is distracting and confusing to have different key messages communicated to your stakeholder groups by various employees from the same company.

I usually introduce my key messages towards the end of my Going Steady meeting to ensure they do not sidetrack me from the information I want to obtain.

Caution

Since you have explained your motive for getting together, you cannot renege and try to sell them something or re-negotiate a contract. If this is done, you will lose all credibility with that contact, and you run the risk of losing credibility with everyone else that person speaks to about the meeting.

It is similar to the basic rules of market research: More than once I have received a phone call at home with a request to conduct some market research. What starts out as a typical survey with a series of questions soon becomes a sales call with the caller obviously trying to sell me something. Any good market researcher will tell you not to switch a market research call into a sales call. In fact, if attempted your reputation will be damaged. Selling is selling and should not be disguised as any other kind of activity.

Another key to success in these meetings is to use effective listening skills. If you are the person doing most of the talking, then you are not gathering information and intelligence. You are, instead, the one *giving* the information. Someone once told me that in general, people like to talk about themselves and their companies. By asking the right questions, you can have an enriching discussion in which you will be able to gather a lot of insight into a particular constituency. I am not suggesting that you simply ask question after question; I am suggesting that you direct the conversation through *effective* questioning. At the end of the meeting, you should not have been the one who has talked the most.

Remember this simple rule: *The person asking the questions is in control of the meeting.*

It is my observation that many people consider themselves effective listeners when, in fact, they are not. Here is a simple test you can apply to determine your own listening effectiveness—I call it the "Fullest Plate Test": The next time you are having a meal with a business colleague, look to see who finishes their meal first. Assuming equivalent portion size and consumption speed, whoever finishes their meal first was the one who was probably doing most of the listening. The one with the fullest plate is the one that was doing most of the talking.

Depending on the circumstance it may be appropriate to be the person doing most of the talking. For example, when I was at a dinner with a group of students I was mentoring from a local university, I hardly touched a bit of my dinner by the time the students had finished their meals. The reason was that the dinner had been arranged for *them* to ask *me* questions about succeeding in business—so they were the ones asking the questions (of which there were many) and I was the one answering to the best of my ability. Needless to say, they controlled our discussion that particular evening.

I also recommend that you do *not* take notes during these meetings unless it is absolutely necessary. You should, instead, make notes immediately following these meetings while the discussion is fresh in your mind.

It is also important to commit to these meetings by not checking your PDA or cell phone in front of the person with whom you are trying to build a Going Steady relationship. People that check their PDA or cell phone during meetings are showing a level of disrespect for whomever they are meeting with. If you are expecting a really important call, then let the person you are meeting with know up front that such a call is expected. Otherwise, leave your PDA/cell phone in your pocket and not on the table.

Once, towards the end of a breakfast with one of our shareholders—*after* business had been conducted—we called a "PDA Time Out". It gave us the chance to mutually check our PDA for a couple of minutes without fear of annoying one another. I thought this was a brilliant way of approaching this issue.

Another essential quality to cultivate in order to obtain the maximum benefit from these relationships is *open-mindedness.* These discussions are not like sales calls where you attempt to handle an objection if you meet opposition or a view contrary to what you expected (or wanted) to hear. Here you want to explore any comments that are contrary or different to your way of thinking. It is perfectly appropriate to probe by asking additional questions to ensure you understand the basis for the different opinion and to test its validity. You don't enter these discussions with a plan to convert everyone to your way of thinking.

One of the very first seminars I attended as a management "newbie" taught me two other very important listening skills that have greatly assisted me over my entire career; these skills also apply to all face-to-face encounters. One of these skills also improves listening during phone calls as well:

1. "It's not *what* you say—it's *how* you say it." Many times a person can tell more by *how* something is being communicated instead of *what* was actually said. This skill requires you to be aware of the tone someone uses when speaking with you, the catchphrases they use, a change in voice pitch or volume, a change in delivery speed, or if they give a long pause before responding. Being sensitive to these behaviours is helpful in both face-to-face meetings and phone calls.

44

2. The second "listening" skill is predominantly visual—it's about body language. Much can be learned from watching the body movements of a person, both while they are speaking and when they are not.

A great deal has been written about both these skills under titles that refer to verbal and non-verbal communications or body language; I strongly recommend that you develop a solid skill set in these two areas.

One of the many important takeaways I gained from the seminar was the ability to not only interpret a *single* occurrence of how someone says something or how their body moves, but to look instead for several repetitions or groupings that support a specific interpretation.

Today, if I sense something from either of these two skill sets when I am in a meeting, I will alter my questioning in order to deal with it. If I have a more senior relationship with someone, I may ask straight out if I sense something is out of line between what they are saying (or I'm saying) and how they are saying it— or what their body language is communicating.

While emailing and social networking provide excellent ways to connect and communicate with people all over the world, your ability to utilize these additional "listening" skills is severely restricted when communicating electronically.

Don't rely on only one type of communication style—use a combination of face-to-face meetings, phone calls, emails, and connections through social networking; choose the style based on what you are trying to achieve.

Just like saving money

At the end of these meetings you will have made substantial deposits into your relationship bank account. However, these deposits must be maintained over time because, unlike a real bank account, if the deposits stop for too long a time then the relationship begins to suffer. Think of it as *negative* interest; if no deposit is made then the balance starts to decline and must be rebuilt before it can progress.

I always think of this as collecting "Brownie points". However, "Brownie points" are fleeting—in fact, they seem to expiry quite quickly, so when you need to make a withdrawal from the

"Brownie point" account, it is often near empty or already has a zero balance—or even worse, it's in the red.

With our relationship accounts we do not want the account balance to decline, and we certainly do not want it to drop to zero. The balance has to be high at all times, so if and *when* we need to make a withdrawal, there is enough in the account to cover it. Remember: *You need a relationship before you need the relationship.*

Just like our bank accounts which are *our* accounts, I think it is important to note that these relationships are *your* responsibility as they are *your* relationships. This means that the onus is on *you* to initiate and maintain these relationships. This is one area where a business relationship differs from a friendship. A *friendship* is a two-way street where both parties will contact each other, each carrying the responsibility to participate in the friendship on more or less equal terms. A *business* relationship may develop into a friendship at some point, but it does not start out that way. Don't be concerned or discouraged if you are the one doing all the work to initiate and maintain your business relationships. The good news about your business relationships is that you are in control of these relationships as you decide who you will have a relationship with and at what level.

Many of today's management courses and books emphasis, as a successful manager, we should control the things we can control. Business relationships are one of the things we can control.

After my first face-to-face meeting where we discussed industry trends, challenges and the future, I look at a six-to nine-month interval before I would arrange a second face-to-face session of this nature. There may be a need to have issue-specific meetings with this person in the interim. Again, the next Going Steady relationship-building meeting would typically be in the form of a breakfast, lunch, or coffee. In between these two face-to-face meetings (assuming no other meetings were scheduled) I would look for an opportunity to touch base at events such as conferences, luncheons, seminars—and also via email by sending information such as interesting industry-related articles or seminar notices. And while I would make sure I was not a pest, I would use these opportunities to just touch base and keep the connection alive. When I send an email, I do not do it as a part of a distribution list; I personalize it specifically to each individual contact. The personal touch is mandatory to convey the importance you place on the relationship you are building with them. I strongly recommend that the emails you send are not forwarded "joke emails"—unless you know the person and their sense of humour extremely well.

After building and maintaining a Going Steady relationship by having a series of these face-to-face meetings with the same subset of multi-stakeholder contacts over a two-year period, I had a very interesting response. At the conclusion of a lunch meeting with one of these individuals, my colleague paid me a completely unsolicited compliment, saying, "I greatly appreciate you taking the time to meet with me; what you do does not go unnoticed and is greatly appreciated." From this I discerned that there had been discussion amongst this subset of multi-stakeholders about my meeting with several of them. More importantly, the mere fact that I was taking the time to meet with this person and the others on a semi-regular basis and talk about industry issues was, in fact, strengthening the brand of our company. It was strengthening our brand not just with this one individual, but with the other multi-stakeholders with whom they had been speaking.

When the lines of communication are open and strong, it is not unusual to receive a communication in between your meetings from someone with whom you have a Going Steady relationship if something has come to their attention that they feel you should be aware of immediately.

We once got a call from a vendor informing us that another one of our vendors from a different industry was planning to go into competition with us. We were not aware of this at the time and were, in fact, in the process of renegotiating a long-term contract with the vendor in question.

This information allowed us to verify the news that the vendor was planning to compete with us; we subsequently ended the relationship with that particular supplier.

If we had not had the Going Steady relationship with that first vendor, we would probably have never received the call, and would have ended up locked into a long-term supply contract with a company that would become a new competitor.

Skill Builder Warm Up:

So far we have identified the stakeholder groups and the individual stakeholder members with whom we would like to build relationships. Additionally, if appropriate, we have enlisted the power of our team of executives who will participate in our relationship-building program, and have identified the stakeholder members for which they will be responsible.

- Now, working with the executive relationship team, identify the two or three topics you want to discuss with each stakeholder group.

- Also identify the two or three key messages you want to deliver about your company when the timing is right. Remember, these key messages should not be sales-oriented.

- Again, if you have not involved others on your executive team, then complete this exercise based on your own network.

But I'm So Busy!

I don't know about you, but in my experience, any time a new responsibility is being introduced to an individual or a group it is not uncommon to hear that it simply cannot be done because everyone is too busy. And they are right—they *are* already very busy.

Alternatively, the new responsibility is reluctantly accepted but is relegated to the very bottom of their priority list and, therefore, never gets done. Many of the executives that might respond with the "I'm too busy" excuse are often seen going to lunch with other staff and/or have very few breakfast meetings.

Let's have a closer look at the actual time commitment needed to maintain those relationships at the Going Steady level:

If your portion of the target senior stakeholder relationship list at the Going Steady level is, for example, twenty external stakeholders and you meet with them twice a year, you need to hold, at a minimum, forty face-to-face meetings. Over the course of any given year let's assume there are two hundred and forty business days, less vacation—let's call it two hundred and twenty business days. With a breakfast and lunch each day, this means there are four hundred and forty opportunities. You only need forty meetings to proactively manage your portion of the senior stakeholder relationship list. If you already have an existing relationship with any of these individuals then the "net new" number of meetings is less.

So, this workload is easily handled without affecting any other corporate priority other than empowering you and your colleagues to make better decisions.

Executives must understand that proactively managing key stakeholder relationships is as important as managing any other aspect of their job.

Companies often pay consultants tens of thousands of dollars to gain this type of input on a one-off basis. Through the adoption of this program, all of this information is available on a continuous basis to you and your team for the cost of a few breakfasts or lunches.

And, if the cost of a few breakfasts or lunches is an obstacle, then simply getting together for a coffee would suffice.

I am not against market research or customer satisfaction surveys; this information can be quite valuable. However, there are two points to consider:

1. Usually, this type of research or surveying is client-based and therefore does not provide input from any other stakeholder group.

2. When researching or surveying your customer base, does it not make more sense to be able to utilize the feedback and information gained from your senior stakeholder relationship sessions when planning your market research or survey?

The use of this information should allow for more focussed and meaningful research and should move you further along the results continuum as opposed to starting, more or less, from scratch.

I experienced a variation on this approach that ultimately led our company to develop a significant new product line:

The head of sales and I were meeting with a client with whom we both had a Courting level relationship. At the end of the meeting, we asked the client if there were any other products or services they thought our firm should be offering that we currently were not. The client answered with a very specific product description and why our company was well-positioned to deliver such a product.

Over the course of a six-month period the head of sales and I asked the same question at the end of our respective client meetings.

When comparing notes after these meetings, we were surprised to find that we were both getting the exact same response from our client base. This led us to include questions on this specific subject in meetings with a subset of our clients with whom we had Going Steady relationships.

At these meetings we validated and clarified the opportunity in this new product space. We were able to identify the combination of factors within the existing marketplace that had been the root cause of the response we had received from our questioning. The combination of poor customer service and quality from the existing providers had become the norm within this market segment. Furthermore, a technological advancement that would revolutionize the industry had occurred but had not been adopted by the current providers.

By identifying all of this information during our Courting and Going Steady relationship meetings, we were able to conduct meaningful and targeted market research—the result of which saw the launch of a very successful new product.

Some of your executives may believe this whole relationship thing is the responsibility of sales; if so, there are a few factors to consider here:

- The senior stakeholder relationship program should span the complete spectrum of stakeholders, not just the client segment which is where sales is focussed.

- The executive level at which the senior relationship program operates would typically be at a higher level, even within the client base, than sales would normally operate.

- Sales staff are hired and trained to pursue a selling cycle and to close a sale. The senior relationship program's objective is to build a long-term sustainable relationship to gain valuable input for enhanced strategic planning and decision-making, not to sell. These are two very different objectives which require different skill sets.

One of the best ways to convince other executives of the merits of a senior relationship program is to show how you have used this technique to better your understanding of differing perspectives of various stakeholders and how this has improved your decision-making and strategic planning participation. An even better way to show the value of this type of program is to also illustrate how others within your executive group have used this type of skill, even though they may not have recognized at the time that they were actually building a senior relationship with a particular stakeholder entity.

Formalizing the process

Remember, everyone already has a number of relationships at various levels. What we are doing, in most cases, is simply taking control of the process, formalizing a current behaviour and, if possible, extending this process across our entire company.

Some may think they do not have the personality to properly participate in this type of activity. Building and maintaining ongoing relationships does not require a gregarious, extroverted personality. These are simple one-on-one meetings with a relatively small group of people; the better prepared we are for these sessions, the easier it will be.

If there is a challenge in this regard, it is usually found in the initial introduction. Those first awkward moments of speaking to someone you have never met before can be rather uncomfortable.

How do you meet a person for the very first time with whom you want to develop a relationship?

There are two types of initial introductions: the ones that we *purposely* make happen, and the ones that happen by *chance*.

For the initial introductions that we purposely make happen, preparation is the name of the game. In the case of a social business function, such as a reception, breakfast, luncheon, or dinner, try to determine ahead of time who will be in attendance. This gives you the opportunity to identify in advance the people you would like to meet with the intention of adding them to your stakeholder-relationship program (and to eventually develop an ongoing relationship at the Going Steady level).

Should a list of attendees not be available in advance, try to create a list of possible attendees and determine which ones you would like to begin building a relationship with.

If there is someone you feel would benefit from attending—and if they are on your list of contacts with whom you'd like to establish a relationship—you could also invite them as your guest. However, it should be noted that, when you have invited a guest to attend a function with you, then your time to network with others is restricted as you will be spending the majority of your time with your guest.

Once we have a target list of names for potential initial introduction, the preparation simply requires finding some background information about the contacts themselves, the company they work for, and their industry. This allows you to make a very significant first impression and allows you to engage in initial small talk that is much more meaningful than talking about the weather or the local sports team.

The better the preparation, the easier the initial introduction—and the better your first impression will be.

Initial introductions that are not pre-planned—instead, happen by chance—occur all the time. For example, during a conference when you are seated at a table for breakfast, lunch or dinner and you do not know everyone at the table, or when someone approaches you at a reception. In fact, sometimes these chance encounters lead to strong ongoing relationships and/or friendships.

Here you may actually begin by talking about the weather or the local sports team. As you have never met this person before—and since he or she is not on your relationship list as of that moment—you have no pre-work to help you. But by having a standard list of questions in the back of your mind, you can carry on a meaningful discourse with virtually anyone.

Here are some standard questions you might include:

- Are you a member of this association?

- If the answer is "Yes", then follow up with an-other question such as, "Have you found this or-ganization useful? If so, then in what way?"

- If they answer "No" when being asked if they are a member of the organization, then follow up with, "What brings you to this particular event?"

Obviously, you should develop a set of questions that you are comfortable with and can call on at a moment's notice in order to initiate or continue a discussion.

In both types of initial introductions you notice, again, the important role asking questions plays. It allows you to control the conversation and it allows the person you are engaged with to talk about themselves, their company and their industry. This allows for a lasting first impression and it provides you with some informa-tion you can utilize later, if you so choose to continue to build the relationship beyond the initial introduction phase.

In all of the above circumstances it is also important to include in your preparation what is commonly known as the "Thirty-Second Elevator Summary" of the business you're in, and the two or three key messages you will deliver at the right moment.

A word of caution: I have noticed at conferences, receptions or any large gatherings the annoying habit many people have of not committing to their conversations. Instead they stand sup-posedly talking to another individual, but all the time their eyes are scanning the crowd and/or checking their PDA. I call this the "Wandering Eye" syndrome. What do you think this behaviour suggests? It suggests that the person with the Wandering Eye is only somewhat engaged in this discussion and is just waiting until they see someone more interesting, or someone more important with whom to connect. It also suggests a lack of respect for the individual with whom they are currently speaking.

I find it very funny to watch two people having a "conversation" with each other when they both suffer from the Wandering Eye syndrome.

To contrast this, my wife and I once had the pleasure of attending a function where Prince Charles was a special guest. It was delightful to see how effortlessly he moved around the room of about two hundred people speaking to each of us individually. When Prince Charles spoke to me his eyes never left mine and he made me feel like I was the only person in the room. He smoothly and graciously engaged and disengaged from each discussion, and made certain he had spoken to everyone.

Now, we may not have the same impact and training on meeting people as does Prince Charles, but I submit to you that if you are diligent to avoid the Wandering Eye syndrome and commit to each discussion, you will leave your colleague feeling important and looking forward to your next encounter.

Remember:

- Be prepared
- Commit to the conversation
- Always maintain eye contact

If you wish to "work the room" or review email, you must disengage from the current conversation at the appropriate time; then, and *only* then, scan the room or check email, and move on.

Another aspect of Formalizing the Process is to do the following:

- Set goals
- Determine next steps
- Set timeframes for developing the relationships you require

These steps should include both developing new relationships and advancing existing relationships.

I actually kept the above list on my desk to act as a constant reminder of what I had to do to begin to proactively manage my relationships. This list also reminded me of the importance business relationships played in the success of my career.

Do not lose an opportunity

Far too often I have seen opportunities missed at conferences, breakfasts, luncheons, and dinners where a group of people attend from the same company and spend the entire time with each other.

They sit together, walk together, eat together, attend the same session together—and very rarely do they ever speak to anyone else, surrounded all the while by business colleagues, clients, prospective clients, suppliers, and other stakeholders. Our natural tendency is to want to spend time with people we know, and usually other staff members are the people we know the best as we probably have spent the most time with them. Still—what a wasted opportunity for establishing new relationships.

Everywhere I have worked in a senior management capacity we had a standing rule of "Divide and conquer." Our staff was not allowed to waste an opportunity at a conference, receptions, or other meetings by spending their time talking to each other.

Skill Builder Warm Up:

- Identify through your own experience where you have benefited from having a relationship at the Going Steady level (even though you may not have recognized it as a Going Steady relationship at the time)

- Identify from internal meetings where you have heard other executives provide input or comment from one of their Going Steady relationships

- Use these examples to build a case for expanding and formalizing a senior relationship program

Remember, everyone on your executive team is already building relationships to one degree or another. This approach is simply making the process more proactive and slightly more formal in order to maximize the benefits to your bottom line.

If the task of doing a compete list for your entire organization is too daunting, then start by either enlisting one or two other executives to join in the program, or prioritize the list yourself and slice the list up into smaller segments and ask the executive to take on responsibility for these relationships. Over time, add another segment until all names on your required relationship list have been assigned.

Set appropriate goals, determine next steps, and set timeframes for each person on your relationship list and determine how and when you will assess your collective progress.

Internal Relationships are Just as Important

We should not overlook the importance of developing the right level of relationships with the key stakeholders within our organizations as well as the external ones. Remember, the section on "You Need a Relationship Before You *Need* the Relationship" applies internally just as it does externally.

Having the right relationships with the right people internally at the right time

- Speeds up the decision-making process
- Reduces the chance of internal politics and
- Provides an effective basis from which differing opinions can be discussed in a non-threatening, non-confrontational manner.

I once had a direct report who would not develop an appropriate-level relationship with his fellow peers (my other direct reports). I noticed over time that whenever this person was presenting a plan, a request for budget/staff, or simply offering an update, there was the greatest amount of discussion and sometimes opposition. Because he had no relationship beyond the Courting level with his peers, he had isolated himself from them—therefore, he had no ability to seek out input, advice, or to gain acceptance (or at least understanding) prior to presenting his plan, budget request or update.

Despite numerous attempts to coach this person to build stronger relationships it was never acted upon, and unfortunately, this person left the organization.

The other direct reports had built Going Steady relationships with each other, resulting in a higher level of collaboration between these individuals; this created much more efficient decision-making.

The Going Steady relationships also gave each of them the comfort level to voice a difference of opinion. When there was a disagreement, which happened often enough, their Going Steady relationship provided a platform to deal with the opposing views that led to better decision-making. However, it is important to note, most potential areas of disagreement were identified in one-on-one meetings prior to executive meetings where they were usually resolved.

Early in my career I was amazed at the number of meetings I would leave where a decision had been taken, only to hear someone who had attended the meeting state an opposing view *which had not been verbalized at the meeting.* This always saddened me because the opportunity to make a better decision had been lost. While there are a number of reasons why someone might withhold opposing views at a meeting, the stronger the level of relationships, the less likely it will occur.

How to Make Internal Relationships Work

Just as I do with my external key stakeholders, I first identify the individuals that are my key internal stakeholders. It is important to remember this list has to be an honest list of key internal stakeholders—not just a list of the people we like.

Secondly, as with my external Going Steady relationships, I meet periodically with my key internal stakeholders to discuss broad corporate initiatives, industry trends and external factors (such as the economy) that impact our business.

I also gain insight into their current successes and challenges in addition to the major projects they are working on. This affords me the opportunity to provide any input I feel is relevant into their thought process, and it allows for any misinterpretations to be addressed quickly. If I have a contrary opinion, it allows for a good discussion in a relaxed setting which typically leads to a better resolution.

For my part, I prepare my two or three key messages that address the major initiatives I am currently working on that at some point will be brought before a larger peer group of which this person is a member.

Again, this provides an opportunity to gain valuable input or a different perspective on an issue and to clear up any misinterpretation. If a differing opinion is identified, it allows for a full, open discussion and potential resolution—or at least a chance to minimize the difference. Quite often this approach will turn a potential adversary into an ally.

Do not be surprised if, by continuously using this approach, you end up managing the group of individuals that were once your peers.

Skill Builder Warm Up:

- Identify your internal key stakeholders and the level of relationship (Initial Contact, Acquaintance, Courting or Going Steady) you currently have with each of them.
- Next, identify the level of relationship you should have with each of them and build a plan to fill the gap.

Make CRM into SRM

Companies spend a lot of time and money developing Customer Relationship Management systems. These systems are vital for sales and customer service departments to monitor, analyze, plan and execute their objectives.

CRM systems also help a company develop a common language when referring to a client and what they are experiencing on the service level or where they are in the selling cycle.

At our company, before we implemented a CRM system, the status of a client in the selling cycle was completely open to interpretation. This meant that when a sales person indicated that a sale was fifty percent closed it was based on what *they* considered that to mean. And, of course, the chance of that meaning the same thing to others was slim.

We also had weekly sales reports that were generated in similar but not identical formats, but these reports were not archived and were certainly not searchable.

The CRM system eliminated these issues because it specifically defined each step in the selling cycle and created an electronic searchable archive. Now, when a sales person says an account is "fifty percent closed," we all know exactly what that means.

These systems also allow for virtually all the staff in the sales and customer service areas to see the history and current status of each and every client and prospect. This has the added benefit of allowing others on the system to see how their colleagues are approaching certain issues, and what is working for them.

Of course, a CRM system is only as good as the quality and completeness of the information that is entered into it, so it is important to create a culture where all the appropriate staff is motivated to keeping the system updated and complete.

As we all know, our client base is only one of our key stakeholder groups. What if we turned our Customer Relationship Management system into a Stakeholder Relationship Management system?

What if we captured all of the details of our discussions with all the stakeholder relationships at the Acquaintance, Courting, and Going Steady levels in our SRM system?

We could reap many of the same benefits we discussed with the CRM system. An SRM system would provide:

- A common language
- An electronic archive
- A searchable database.

Think of the power of being able to see how a specific topic of discussion that had been identified for the Going Steady relationship level was progressing as the various meetings were being conducted. Consider the efficiency gained by the system automatically reminding us when it was time to set up another meeting with a particular person.

Of course, because of the highly sensitive nature of this information, access should be restricted to the appropriate people.

If it is not possible to expand your customer relationship system to a stakeholder relationship system, then at least follow the *theory* of the CRM. Make sure you have a way (for each of the relationship levels) of capturing activities and findings and for sharing this information within the group that is participating in the senior stakeholder relationship program.

Skill Builder Warm Up:

- Identify the type of information you want to maintain on your list of key stakeholders.
- Investigate the CRM system used by your company and determine how it could be expanded to include your senior stakeholder relationship requirements identified above.
- If this is not possible, then create a method of maintaining and updating the required information, sharing it with other participants in your senior stakeholder relationship program.

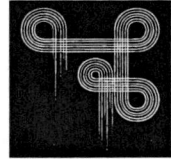

Social Media, Social Networking and Relationships

Social media, social networking and online communications are powerful tools to have in our relationship management tool kit. But we must understand where and when they are effective, and how to use them correctly.

Social media/networking platforms provide good opportunities to enhance our ability to expand our Initial Contact group. These platforms provide fast and easy ways to introduce ourselves to others without geographic or time zone restrictions. Once you are a part of these communities, they typically allow you to leverage existing relationships as a way of introduction to others.

Social media/networks also allow you to progress a relationship from the Initial Contact level to the Acquaintance level through continued online dialogue and through the use of questions. However, the same rules apply when building a relationship in a social media/network as in the face-to-face world.

It is important not to misrepresent yourself or your intentions when building relationships in this space. A typical example occurs when someone has been accepted into a social media/ network community and then begins aggressively selling a product or service. This does *not* end well for this individual, as they are usually dealt with quite harshly by the group or its administrator.

In the case where a social media/networking platform includes high-level technology, it may be possible to grow a relationship up to the Courting level.

The real-time video aspect is important because, at this level of relationship, trust still must be cultivated; the ability to see body language and to hear tonality plays a vital role in building this trust.

The people I have consulted with and whom I consider experts in this field say it would be difficult to build a Going Steady level relationship solely through social media/networking. I believe the true power of relationship-building comes from using a combination of face-to-face, social media/networking, telephone and traditional online (email).

Many times after a face-to-face meeting we have all received the obligatory "Thank you for meeting" email. It usually contains nothing more than a "Thank you for your time, great to see you again," etc.

For a Going Steady-level relationship, send an email after a meeting that goes beyond "Thank you" and says how much you appreciate the person sharing their views with you. You do not need to be detailed as to what specific views they stated.

By simply referencing the topics you discussed, you will help the person commit their views to memory; additionally, they will remember how beneficial the meeting was to them, because you asked them for their opinion and took them seriously.

Social media/networking and online communication allows you to easily keep in touch with your senior business relationships between face-to-face meetings.

If you happen to find an interesting news article, research paper, or webcast, you can use social media/networking and online communications to pass the information along to the appropriate segment of your network.

Be careful not to list out all your contact names in the address line of your email unless you really want to. If you want to make someone feel special, then do not show their name on a distribution list. Instead, take a little time and address each email individually.

Are Relationships Your Competitive Advantage or Your Competitors?

If you are not building the senior-level relationships you need to succeed, then someone else may be doing it *instead* of you. This someone could be from your company or, even worse, from a competitor.

If the "someone else" is from your company, then while your company will benefit from the strategic relationships developed, *you* may not be as successful in your career at that company as will your colleague who developed their relationships.

If the "someone else" is from a competitor, then there is a double loss; not only will *you* not succeed to your fullest potential, the success of *your company* may also be limited.

In many cases—sales being the obvious exception—there is minimal downside risk to both you and your competitor having a senior (Courting or Going Steady) relationship with the same stakeholder. In fact, sometimes it may be a benefit, as you might inadvertently learn something about your competitors while in discussion with a stakeholder. The risk is that some of *your* discussion points could be passed along to your competitor. My own experience suggests it is usually the person with the most senior relationship who is more likely to be the recipient of competitive information.

Just because you decide *not* to develop strategic relationships does not mean they will not be developed—it just means that they may be developed by *someone else*. Do not put the strategic relationship "secret weapon" solely into the hands of your competitor.

It is never too late to begin to develop strategic relationships even if you are the second or third one to come to the party.

Skill Builder Warm Up:

- Using the stakeholder list you developed earlier, review each of the stakeholder groups and again, being brutally honest, identify the stakeholders where you know your competitor has a senior-level relationship.

- Based on your list of priority stakeholders, determine if you need to develop a higher-level relationship with any of these individuals.

What it All Boils Down To

It comes down to choice. You can choose to continue with your relationships at the levels you already have, or you can choose to change the way you approach relationships and increase your likelihood of success.

The reasons for change are compelling as the right level of relationship with the right stakeholders at the right time can improve:

- A company's brand
- A company's market position/reputation
- Corporate decision-making
- The quality of the strategic and annual plans
- The quality of market research
- The level of corporate exposure
- The crisis management and risk management processes.

Additionally, you will personally benefit from participating by:

- Enhancing your own personal brand
- Further strengthening your credibility and reputation
- Expanding your personal knowledge base
- Making better, more informed decisions
- Becoming a better strategic planner
- Expanding your career opportunities.

All these benefits can be realized with minimal effort and minimal additional cost.

Even better, all this can be achieved—or at least improved upon—with very little change to your current behaviour. You already have a number of relationships at the Initial Contact,

Acquaintance, Courting or Going Steady levels, so much of the work is already in place.

The best news is that you can scale a strategic relationship management program to fit your specific situation starting with your own relationships and stakeholder contacts. When you are ready, you can expand this program to include a small group of your colleagues, and eventually to an entire senior management team.

Remember to commit to the Three Right Rule and ensure you have the right level of relationship with the right people (your key stakeholder groups) at the right time.

And, you truly have to be (or become) a good listener.

Once this is accomplished you will be unstoppable.

While you are busy identifying, building and maintaining your own relationships, be aware of people who are trying to build and maintain a relationship with *you*. Of course, you do not have the time to have a high-level relationship (Courting or Going Steady levels) with *everyone* who reaches out to you, so selectivity is important.

A person who was not on my list of key stakeholders had, over the years, built a Going Steady-level relationship with me. We had many interesting and thought-provoking conversations which had always been initiated by this other individual. As our relationship progressed, I was asked to sit on the board of directors of a company he was involved with.

I am glad this person had put me on their list of people they wanted to have a Going Steady relationship with as I have truly benefited from this experience.

Relationships—the benefits are many, the requirements are minimal, and in the final analysis, *business relationships are key to your success.*

Now it's all up to you.

Good luck!

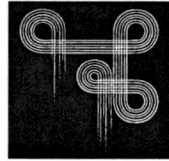

Key Points – Glossary of Terms and Definitions

Stakeholder **Relationships allow a company** to improve decision-making and strategic planning, build a stronger brand, improve crisis management effectiveness, enhance market research and gain greater exposure of its key messages.

Stakeholder relationships allow an individual to increase reputation, credibility and knowledge base; improve their participation in strategic planning; build a stronger personal brand; and make better, more informed decisions.

A **Stakeholder** is any group that can seriously impact your business, or whose business your company can seriously impact.

Initial Contact is the first meeting where the initial exchange of business cards (or electronic exchange) usually occurs. In either case, there must be an exchange of meaningful dialogue which must occur within twelve months of initial contact. Remember the **Desperate High School Student Syndrome.**

Acquaintance: These are people you see at conferences, dinners, receptions, etc. You know each other's names and exchange small talk but had never had a real business meeting.

Courting: This level comprises the group of individuals where we have had one or two sales meetings or issue-specific meetings, the most recent of these meeting having been within the last twelve months.

Going Steady: This level consists of the group of individuals you meet with on a regular or semi-regular basis where you discuss broader industry trends, directions, and more.

The Three Right Rule: The right level of relationship with the right stakeholders at the right time.

The **quality of input and the level of trust**—shown *to* you and shown *by* you—varies directly with the level of relationship.

You need a relationship before you ***need*** the relationship.

Not having the right relationships with the right stakeholders at the right time creates **Input Isolation** which restricts decision-making and planning abilities.

The person that asks the questions is the person that controls a meeting. Prepare questions in advance of the meeting.

Listening: Are you really a good listener, or a "Got One Better" listener? Remember the **Fullest Plate Test**.

Relationship Layering avoids biases, personality conflicts and Sole Face Syndrome. It also validates input.

Relationship Plateau occurs when we believe we have all the relationships we need, and we stop or pause in the active management of our existing relationships and in the development of new Courting or Going Steady relationships.

Leverage the **Connected People, the Spokespeople, and the Multi-stakeholder People**.

Timing of relationships and keeping them current is everything.

If you're tempted to say "but I'm too busy," remember that Going Steady relationships *only require two meetings each per year.*

$$E \ m \ c^2$$

Enright Management Coaching & Consulting Inc. (Emc2) provides an unique approach of combining coaching and consulting. Our goal is to be sure that, once an assignment is completed, our client has not only achieved their desired result—such as a strategic plan—they have also developed the skills necessary to complete this exercise for themselves in the future.

This combination of coaching and consulting provides our clients with long-term cost control, skill development, and knowledge transfer, creating a greater commitment by the client to obtain the desired results.

Of course, either straight consulting or coaching assignments are always available.

Emc2 provides benefit and expertize in the following areas:

Strategic Planning	**Product Development**
Sales & Prospecting	**Marketing & Communications**
Presentation Skills	**Relationship Management**
Succession Planning	**Board of Directors Training**

For more information on Enright Management Coaching & Consulting Inc. please visit enrightconsulting.ca.

About the Author

Tom Enright is a proven leader with extensive C-suite, independent director and board experience with public and private companies and not-for-profits. His work experience spans over thirty years with organizations such as The Toronto Stock Exchange, The Financial Post, CNW Group (Canada Newswire) and the Canadian Investor Relations Institute.

In addition, he has been Deputy Chairman, Chairman, Independent Director and also member of Audit Committee and Chair of Compensation Committee on various private and public company boards.

Tom is Chairman and CEO of Enright Management Coaching & Consulting Services Inc. and also provides mentoring services to individuals and companies through Executive Mentors. He has also presented and conducted workshops on strategic planning, sales and marketing, and relationship management throughout Canada, the United States, the United Kingdom and Asia.

In addition to writing *Business Relationships: Key to Your Success*, he is also an occasional columnist to various publications and contributing author to Andy Higgins' book entitled *Best Coaches, Best Practices*.

Tom received an Arbor Award from the University of Toronto in 2003, the University of Toronto Scarborough Alumni Award in 2004, and was the first Honorary Chair of the University of Toronto at Scarborough Mentorship Program.

In 2008, he was awarded the Lifetime Achievement Award in investor relations by IR Magazine and in 2012 received an Honorary Lifetime membership in the Canadian Investor Relations Institute.

The author lives in Toronto with his wife Linda, and close to their two amazing children Matthew (and wife Lauren), Courtney (and husband Noah) and granddaughter Piper Grace.

CPSIA information can be obtained at www.ICGtesting.com
Printed in the USA
LVOW13s2051120713

342689LV00001B/6/P